The Little Bug

written by Jay Dale

illustrated by Anna Hancock

"Look!" said Min Monkey.
"I can see a little bug.
The little bug
is red and black."

"Come here,"
said Grandpa Tut.
"The little bug is hiding."

"Come on, little bug," said Min Monkey. "We can play."

"No!" said Grandpa Tut.
"The little bug is hiding.
It can see
a big black spider."

"*Eeeeeekkkkk!*"
cried Min Monkey.
"I can see
a big black spider, too.
It is coming after me!"

"No!" said Grandpa Tut.
"You are
a silly little monkey.
The big black spider
is **not** coming after you.
It is coming after
the little bug."

"Oh!" said Min Monkey.
"Come here, little bug.
I will look after you."

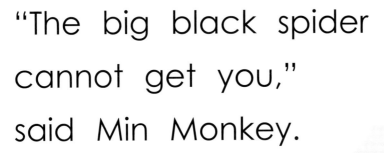

"The big black spider cannot get you," said Min Monkey.